Down the Road

Down the Road

Alice Schertle

ILLUSTRATED BY

E.B. Lewis

DEVELOPMENTAL STUDIES CENTER

This Developmental Studies Center edition is published by arrangement
with Houghton Mifflin Harcourt Publishing Company.

Developmental Studies Center
1250 53rd Street, Suite 3
Emeryville, CA 94608-2965
800.666.7270 * fax: 510.464.3670
devstu.org

ISBN 978-1-61003-184-4
Printed in China

1 2 3 4 5 6 7 8 9 10 RRD 20 19 18 17 16 15 14

The paintings in this book were done in Winsor & Newton
watercolors on 300-lb. D'Arches cold-press paper.
The display type was set in Recklman Solid.
The text type was set in Palatino by Thompson Type, San Diego, California.
Designed by Camilla Filancia

For Dave and Ree

— A. S.

To Hasan, my first son

— E. B. L.

Hetty lived in a little gray house with a big stone chimney and a screen door that squeaked in a friendly way for comings and goings.

In back of the house was a tin-roof shed, where Papa mended other people's trucks and tractors, and cars that weren't running anymore.

In front of the house was a dusty road that ran through a field, up over a hill, and out of sight.

Sometimes Hetty walked with Mama down the dusty road. Sometimes she walked with Papa. But Hetty had never, ever been allowed down the dusty road all by herself.

One afternoon Mama said, "Mr. Birdie's speckled hens are laying. Wouldn't fresh eggs be nice for tomorrow's breakfast?" She sighed and shook her head. "I just don't have time to walk to Mr. Birdie's. It's too bad."

"Scrambled eggs for breakfast!" said Papa. "If only I had the time, I'd go myself."

"I can do it," said Hetty. "I'm big enough to go to Mr. Birdie's all by myself."

"Well . . . ," said Mama.

"Look at this big girl," said Papa. "Hetty can do it, Mama. Absolutely."

Papa gave Hetty a handful of coins and a wicker basket. "One dozen eggs," he told her. "Twelve big beauties. No cracks."

"Be sure to say thank you to Mr. Birdie," said Mama.

"Come straight home," said Papa.

"Don't dillydally," said Mama.

Squeak-bang! went the screen door, and Hetty was on her way.

She marched straight down the dusty road, swinging the basket and jingling the coins in her pocket. *This is what it's like to be grown-up,* she thought. *You have money in your pocket, and you can go down the road all by yourself.*

She listened to her shoes going *thup, thup, thup, thup,* and she made up some walking words to say as she went along:

> Down the road,
> one and two,
> eggs for breakfast,
> how-de-do!

> Eggs for breakfast,
> *clickety-clack,*
> eggs for breakfast,
> not a *crack!*

Bump! went the basket against Hetty's knee. *Bump! Bump!*

When this basket is full of eggs, thought Hetty, *I'll walk my smoothest so they won't roll around and break.*

She practiced walking as if she were skimming across a frozen pond on ice skates. Pretty soon her walk was so smooth that she balanced the wicker basket on her head and climbed all the way to the top of the hill before it fell off.

With the basket over her arm, Hetty raced down the other side, her pigtails flying.

She felt inside her pocket to make sure the coins were still there. Then she continued down the road . . . through a meadow . . . across a stream . . .

past a house or two . . . down a street . . . around a corner . . . up some steps . . .

. . . and into the cool shadows of Mr. Birdie's Emporium and Dry Goods Store.

"Well, now," said Mr. Birdie, "here's Hetty, all by herself."

"Good day, Mr. Birdie," said Hetty, just as Mama would have said. "I'd like a dozen eggs, please." She slapped the coins down on the counter, just as Papa would have done. "Twelve big beauties. No cracks."

While Mr. Birdie put twelve big brown eggs into the wicker basket, Hetty walked slowly down a cluttered aisle, looking closely at cans and cartons and bolts of fabric, just as if she might decide to buy something else.

Before she left, she remembered to say, "Thank you, Mr. Birdie."

Around the corner went Hetty, down the street, past a house or two, doing her smooth walk and holding the basket carefully so it wouldn't bump against her knees. When she came to the stream, she stopped with one foot on a fallen log.

What if it wobbles? thought Hetty. *What if this log wobbles me off and I drop the eggs?* She stepped down into the cold water and splashed across the stream, straight across to the other side. *No use taking a chance,* thought Hetty.

Squish, squish, went Hetty's wet shoes on the dusty road. *Squish, squish, squish, squish,* and Hetty said her walking words:

Down the road,
one and two,
eggs for breakfast,
how-de-do!

Hetty was so busy doing her smooth walk, and saying her walking words, and admiring the eggs in the basket that she didn't see a rock sticking up in the middle of the road. She walked along, getting closer to the rock with every step.

Eggs for breakfast,
clickety-clack,
eggs for breakfast
not a—OUCH!

Hetty's toe hit the rock, and she stumbled forward. She had to hop and jump to keep from falling. Inside the basket the eggs rattled together with little clinky sounds.

"Oh, no!" said Hetty. She knelt down on the road and took the eggs out of the basket. Scarcely breathing, she examined every one.

"Not a crack," she said with a sigh. She wiped each egg off on her shirt and put them all back inside.

Then she was on her way again, *this* time keeping a sharp eye out for obstacles on the road.

It seemed like a very long road. The sun was hot, and by the time she reached the meadow, Hetty was tired. But there, in the middle of the meadow, was a big wild apple tree, full of bright red apples. Sweet, juicy, crackly-crisp apples.

Papa's favorites. Mama's, too. Hetty herself was very fond of apples. *Just three*, thought Hetty, *and then I'll go straight home.* She made her way through the weeds, snagging foxtails in her socks and holding the egg basket carefully in front of her.

Hetty picked an apple for Mama. She picked an apple for herself. Now for a big, red, Papa-size apple. She reached up . . . up . . . and the wicker basket tipped just a little bit. She reached higher . . . higher . . . and the basket tipped a little more . . . a little more. . . .

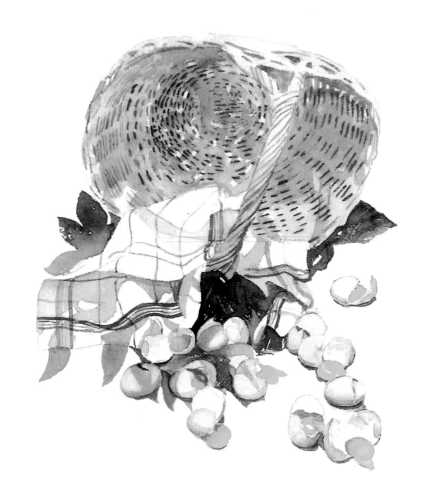

SPLAT!

Hetty wanted to cry. She wanted to hide. She wanted to climb up into the apple tree and never, ever come down.

She *didn't* want to go home and tell Papa and Mama there would be no eggs for breakfast.

Up she climbed, right up into the old apple tree, as high as she could go.
And there she sat, just thinking, and feeling sad, and not wanting to go home.

After a long time Hetty saw something moving, way down the dusty road.

It was Papa. Hetty made herself as small as she could. Papa, whose sharp eyes never missed a thing, came striding through the tall meadow grass.

"So!" he said. "This is where I find you. Is this how you bring eggs home for breakfast?"

"I was picking apples for us," said Hetty with a sob. "I broke the eggs, Papa. Every single one."

Papa nudged the basket with the toe of his boot. "I see," he said. "And you climbed up into the tree to think it over." Suddenly his face wrinkled into a smile. "There's no finer place than an apple tree to think things over." And Papa climbed up beside her.

By the time Mama came
through the meadow grass, there
was a pile of apple cores under-
neath the tree. Hetty and Papa
had chins sticky with apple juice.

Mama nudged the basket
with the toe of her shoe. "Just
look at this! I'm waiting for twelve
beautiful eggs, and what do I find?
Shells!"

"I'm sorry, Mama," said Hetty.
"I dropped the eggs. I was trying
to pick some apples—"

"Fine, sweet apples," said
Papa.

Mama stared up into the
tree. "Well, well," she said. "Just
look at the two big birds in the
apple tree."

Papa whistled like a magpie
"Tweet, tweet, tweet," went Hetty.

Pretty soon there were three big birds in the apple tree.

Mama put her arm around Hetty. "I'd almost forgotten how lovely the world looks from a tree," Mama said.

"Everyone should spend some time in an apple tree," Papa agreed. "Absolutely."

When they walked back home along the dusty road, they had not one egg among them. But Mama's skirt, and Papa's pockets, and Hetty's basket were full of sweet red apples.

And the next morning . . . there was apple pie for breakfast.